Adventure with Fractions

Book Four of
The Gift of Numbers
Math Fantasy Curriculum

Rachel Rogers and Joe Lineberry

Illustrations by ARTE RAVE

gic Formula #204

1/3 apple pie

1/4 chocolate bar

3 dandelion leaves

1 1/2 cups goat's milk

end all ingredents in a blender. Makes thre
servings.

Prospective Press Academics

an imprint of

PROSPECTIVE PRESS LLC

1959 Peace Haven Rd, #246, Winston-Salem, NC 27106 U.S.A.
www.prospectivepress.com

Published in the United States of America by PROSPECTIVE PRESS LLC

ADVENTURE WITH FRACTIONS

Text copyright © Rachel Rogers and Joe Lineberry, 2020
All rights reserved.
The authors' moral rights have been asserted.

Illustrations by ARTE RAVE
© Prospective Press, 2020
All rights reserved.
The illustrator's moral rights have been asserted.

ISBN 978-1-943419-54-8

ProP-F009

Adventure with Fractions is the fourth volume in the Gift of Numbers math fantasy curriculum. For information on additional volumes in the series or for bulk sales, please send inquiries to education@prospectivepress.com

Printed in the United States of America
First paperback printing November, 2020

The text of this book is typeset in Mouse Memoirs
Accent text is typeset in Galindo

PUBLISHER'S NOTE

This book is a work of creative non-fiction with fictional fantasy elements. The people, names, characters, locations, activities, and events portrayed or implied by this book are the product of the author's imagination or are used fictitiously. Any resemblance to actual people, locations, and events is strictly coincidental. No actual pollution occurred in this book.

Without limiting the rights as reserved in the above copyright, no part of this publication may be reproduced, stored in or introduced into any retrieval system, or transmitted–by any means, in any form, electronic, mechanical, photocopying, recording, or otherwise–without the prior written permission of the publisher. Not only is such reproduction illegal and punishable by law, but it also hurts the authors and illustrator who toiled hard on the creation of this work and the publisher who brought it to the world. In the spirit of fair play, and to honor the labor and creativity of the authors and illustrator, we ask that you purchase only authorized electronic and print editions of this work and refrain from participating in or encouraging piracy or electronic piracy of copyright-protected materials. Please give creators a break and don't steal this or any other work.

Dedicated to our inspiring parents:

Rachel's mama and daddy

Alice

Jabe

Joe's mom and dad

Nina

J.L.

"We have exciting news," said Reporter 9 News. "Today number 3 vanished. His fact family, numbers 9 and 12, had gone shopping. They were not there to use a math operation to bring him back. You know, they could not subtract 12 – 9 = 3."

"Later he re-appeared at his house anyway. He had no help from his fact family. So tell me, number 3, how long were you gone?"

Number 3 was still in a daze. His friend, King Less, was with him. "I think I was gone a half hour," mumbled number 3.

Reporter News did some quick math. "Let's see, sixty minutes is a whole hour. If I divide sixty minutes into two equal parts, that would be two parts of thirty minutes. 30 + 30 = 60. You were gone thirty minutes. What did you see while you were gone?"

"I remember looking down on a world of girls and boys," said number 3. "I was floating in the air with a lot of different numbers. The girls and boys couldn't see us, but I could see them."

"Then what happened?" Reporter News asked.

"I watched for several minutes. Then I felt really tired. I yawned, and suddenly I was back at my house in Odd Nation," said number 3.

"Wow! What a dream! That sounds scary," exclaimed King Less.

"We must stop our numbers from disappearing. If we don't stop this, future boys and girls will run out of numbers," said King Less. "I know how. I'm going to get a magic formula from the Dream Princess. I heard she sells formulas to make dreams come true. Do you want to come along?"

"Sure," they replied. "How do we get there?"

King Less replied, "We start at the main bridge. We walk on the dirt road until it splits in half. We take the right half to the mountains."

"How long does it take to get there?" asked Reporter News.

"It takes thirty minutes," said King Less. "Let's meet at the bridge at 10:00."

Reporter News put his fingers on his chin. "Let me think," he said. "We leave at 10:00 and it takes thirty minutes to get there. We should be there at 10:30."

The three numbers met at the bridge and walked on the dirt road. They came to the place where it split in half. The road was divided into two equal parts. One half of the road went left, and one half of the road went right.

"Let's see," said King Less, holding up his right hand. "We take the right half of the road to the mountains."

As they turned right, Reporter News said, "This will be a great story. Only a few numbers have ever seen Dream Princess. What do we look for now?"

"There it is, in the distance." said King Less. "See the sign on the side of the mountain: 'Dream Princess—Magic Formulas and Computer Repairs.'"

King Less continued, "Look at the other sign: 'Today Only—Magic Formulas Half Price.' This is our lucky day!"

Number 3 looked puzzled. "What does that mean—half price?" he asked.

Reporter News spoke up, "That means the price of any magic formula is half of the normal price. If a magic formula normally costs $10, you divide $10 into two equal parts. That is $10 = $5 + $5. So today's price is $5, one half the normal $10 price."

$10 = $5 + $5

When the three adventurers arrived at Dream Princess's store, the princess walked out to meet them. King Less was shocked when he saw her. "You're . . . you're . . . you're a ghostly zero!" stammered King Less.

"Well, yes I am," said the princess. "Is that a problem?"

"Maybe," said King Less. "Our numbers didn't disappear until a ghostly zero showed up."

"Yes, I heard that. This occurred after I gave King More a dream about addition and after you had an idea about subtraction," replied Dream Princess. She paused and added, "I thought you might come to me for a magic formula." She turned around and walked into her store.

Inside the store the princess stood behind the counter. The three adventurers were staring at a thick, musty book in her hands. The title of the book was *Magic Formulas for Magicians*.

Dream Princess plopped the book on the counter. She opened it and asked the group, "How can I help you?"

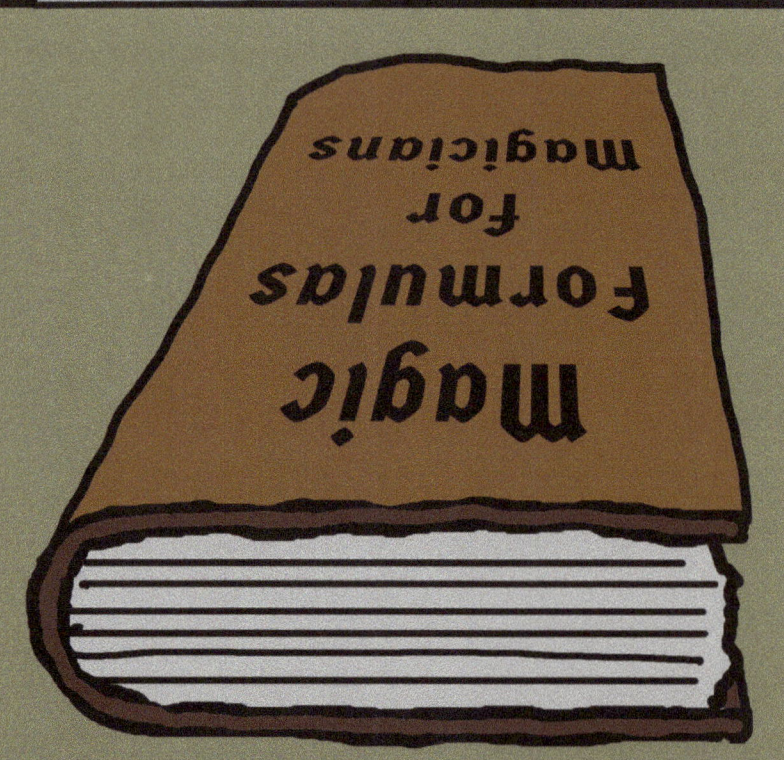

"So you are a magician. That's great! Our numbers have been disappearing," said King Less. "We need a magic formula that keeps them from disappearing."

"Really?" said the princess. "You don't want your numbers to disappear. Is that right?"

"Of course, we don't want them to disappear," said King Less. "It's scary to disappear."

"We have a problem," said Dream Princess. "I don't remember if I have a formula that keeps a number from disappearing. I do have a formula to help numbers re-appear after disappearing."

"Okay," said King Less hopefully. "What does your book say about helping numbers re-appear?"

"I always remember where that magic formula is located," explained the princess, as she started turning pages. "It is halfway through my book. This book has 400 pages, so I divide it into two equal parts. 200 + 200 = 400. So it is on page 200."

"Ah! Here it is. All the book says about re-appearing is 'Yawn.' No magic formula is needed. After you vanish, you just yawn and then you re-appear."

YAWN

Note: Page 200 is halfway through my book. Page 200 is half the 400 pages of the book.

King Less, Reporter News, and number 3 looked at each other, wondering what was going on. "That's what happened to me," recalled number 3. "I yawned and suddenly I was back at my house in Odd Nation."

Dream Princess was so focused on her book that she did not hear them talking. She turned back one page. "And here on page 199 is a magic formula to help numbers disappear. We make a lot of this formula."

"We have many numbers wanting to disappear," continued the princess. "The problem is this magic formula doesn't work well after two days. When it spoils, we throw the leftover formula into the river. Then we use the recipe to make a new batch."

Dream Princess kept turning pages. "Wait!" she exclaimed. "I was wrong. I do have a magic formula to keep numbers from disappearing."

King Less was so excited that he was trembling. "Are you kidding? What does it say?" he yelled.

"Relax," said the princess. "I can't promise it will work. I have never made this magic formula before. You can look at the recipe here on page 204. It shows the directions and a picture of each ingredient."

They all leaned over to look at the wrinkled page. "Finally!" exclaimed King Less. "We can keep our numbers from disappearing. Future boys and girls will not run out of numbers to use."

The princess tried to speak, "I don't think you understand how this works..."

King Less interrupted her, "No more talking. Let's make this magic formula."

Magic Formula #204

 1/3 apple pie

 1/4 chocolate bar

 3 dandelion leaves

 1 1/2 cups goat's milk

Blend all ingredients in a blender. Makes three servings.

How to Prevent Numbers from Disappearing

Dream Princess pulled out a large blender and an apple pie. She made a small hole in the middle of the pie. Then from the middle she drew three lines. Following those lines, she sliced the pie into three equal parts.

"Look," said Reporter News to number 3. "She is cutting it like a 'Y.' Now she has three equal parts. Each piece is 1/3 of the pie."

The princess put one piece of pie into the blender. Next she grabbed a chocolate candy bar off the shelf. She unwrapped it and reached for her knife. She cut it into four equal parts. One part equaled one fourth of the chocolate bar, so she put one part into the blender.

The third step was easy. She picked out three dandelion leaves and dropped them into the blender.

Dream Princess pulled a container of goat's milk out of the refrigerator. She poured one whole cup of milk into the blender. Then she poured one-half cup of milk into the blender.

All the ingredients were in the blender, so she turned the blender on.

Number 3 glanced at the recipe again. "What does this mean, 'Makes three servings?'"

The princess turned off the blender and pulled out three glasses. She replied, "That means this recipe makes enough for three of you to share. See the lines on the blender. They divide the liquid in the blender into three equal servings. You each can drink 1/3 of this magic formula."

She poured 1/3 of the formula into each glass. Each of the adventurers took a gulp from his glass. "Wow!" exclaimed number 3. "How can anything this sugary be good for you?"

While the king was paying for the magic formula, Reporter News looked out the window. "Are there any other numbers living in the mountains with you?" he asked.

"Oh, yes," said Dream Princess. "We have many numbers living around here—odd numbers and even numbers."

"That's interesting," said King Less. "Do odd numbers and even numbers work together and live together, like we do in Odd Nation and Even Land?"

"Of course," said the princess. "They play together, too—football and many other games. You can't see a lot of the numbers. Many of them decided to disappear for a while."

"Disappear?"

King Less turned to Reporter News and number 3. "We need to get out of here. These mountain numbers want to disappear."

King Less grabbed the recipe. The three adventurers rushed out the door and hurried home.

Adventure with Fractions Exercise

1. Dream Princess has an apple pie, a blueberry pie, and a cherry pie. As you follow these instructions, remember fractions are equal parts.

    a. Divide the apple pie into halves:

    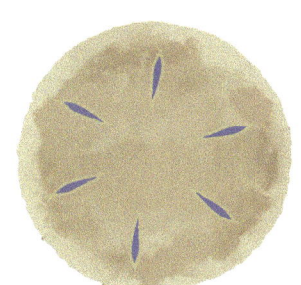

    b. Divide the blueberry pie into thirds:

    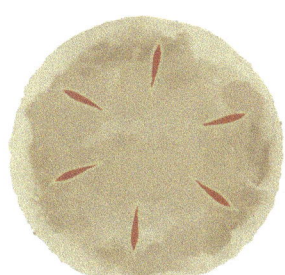

    c. Divide the cherry pie into fourths:

2. Dream Princess pulled out three chocolate bars. Show three different ways to divide the chocolate bars into fourths.

How do you know the bars are divided into fourths?

The Publisher hereby grants permission to the original purchaser and/or sole owner of this book to make copies of this page for in-class use only. Copies may not be transmitted, sold, lent, or stored–electronically or otherwise.

3. Reporter News used a clock to plan his trip. Write a fraction to describe equal parts of the clock.

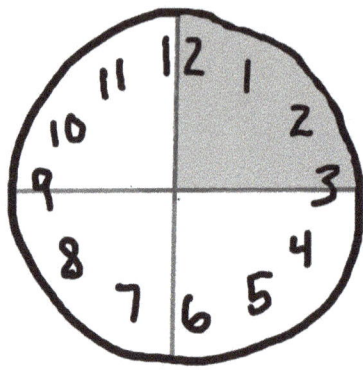

a. How many parts are gray? ☐

b. How many equal parts is the clock divided into? ☐

c. What fraction of the clock is gray? ☐/☐

4. Are the parts of King Less's crown equal or unequal? Circle the correct answer.

a. Equal or Unequal

b. Equal or Unequal

c. Equal or Unequal

Discussion Questions

1. Why was King Less surprised when he saw Dream Princess?

2. Using details from the story, find three examples of fractions.

3. Why do you think the authors wrote *Adventure with Fractions*?

4. Summarize the story, *Adventure with Fractions*. Tell the important events in the beginning, in the middle, and at the end of the story.

Exercise Solutions

1. a.
   b.
   c.

2.

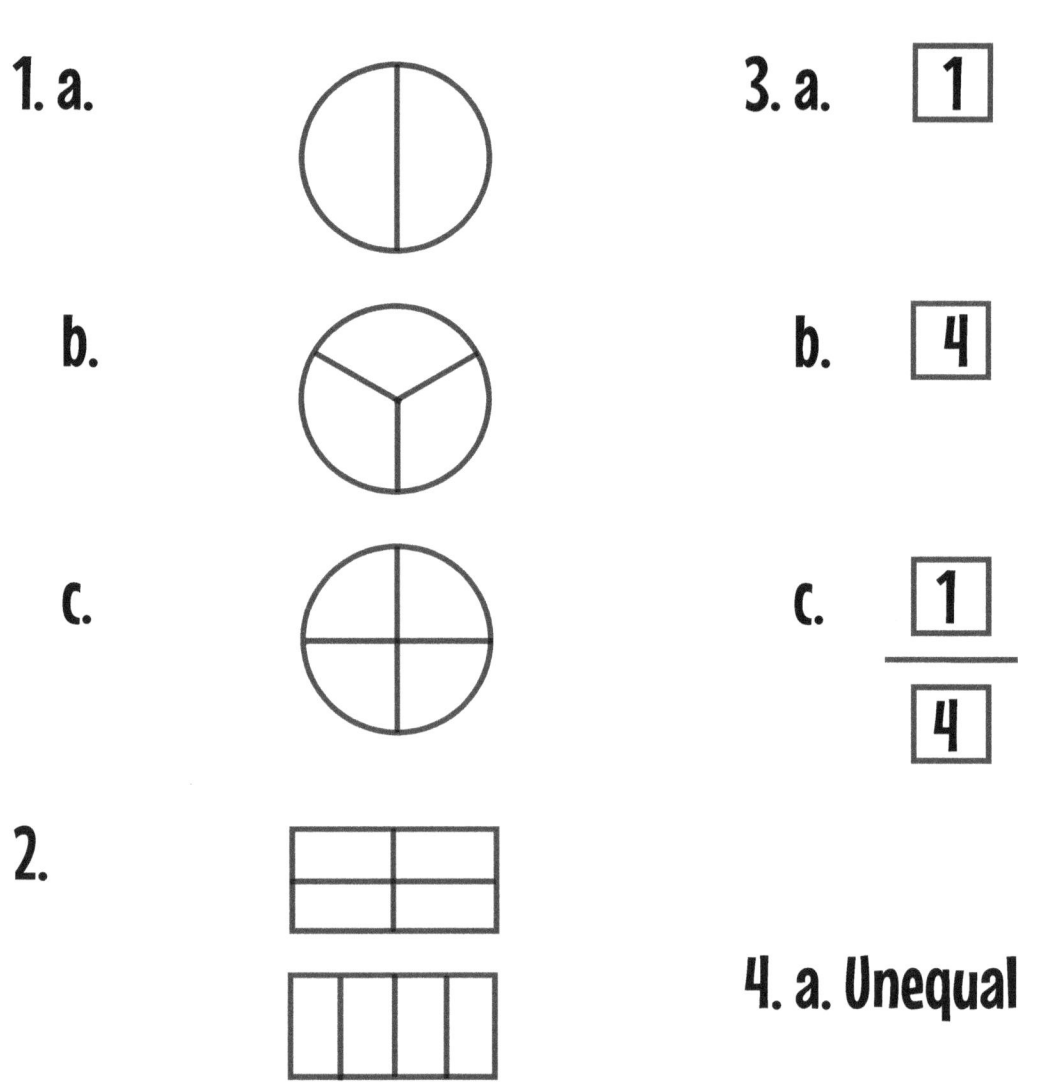

I know the chocolate bars are divided into fourths because there are four parts and all parts are equal.

3. a. $\boxed{1}$

   b. $\boxed{4}$

   c. $\dfrac{\boxed{1}}{\boxed{4}}$

4. a. Unequal

   b. Equal

   c. Unequal

About the Authors

Rachel Rogers
is an elementary school teacher at Old Richmond Elementary School, Winston-Salem, NC. She has more than 35 years of experience teaching first, second, and third graders.

Joe Lineberry
told similar stories to his sons when they were growing up. He is also the author of *Let's Stop Playing Games: Finding Freedom in Authentic Living*.

About the Books

The Gift of Numbers
is a math fantasy curriculum that combines literature and mathmatics in a fun, age-appropriate series for second- and third-grade students.

   Volume 1: *Saved by Addition*
   Volume 2: *Surprised by Subtraction*
   Volume 3: *Graphing the Mystery*
   Volume 4: *Adventure with Fractions*
   Volume 5: *Multiplication Football*
   Volume 6: *The Experiment Game*
   Volume 7: *Division Gymnastics*